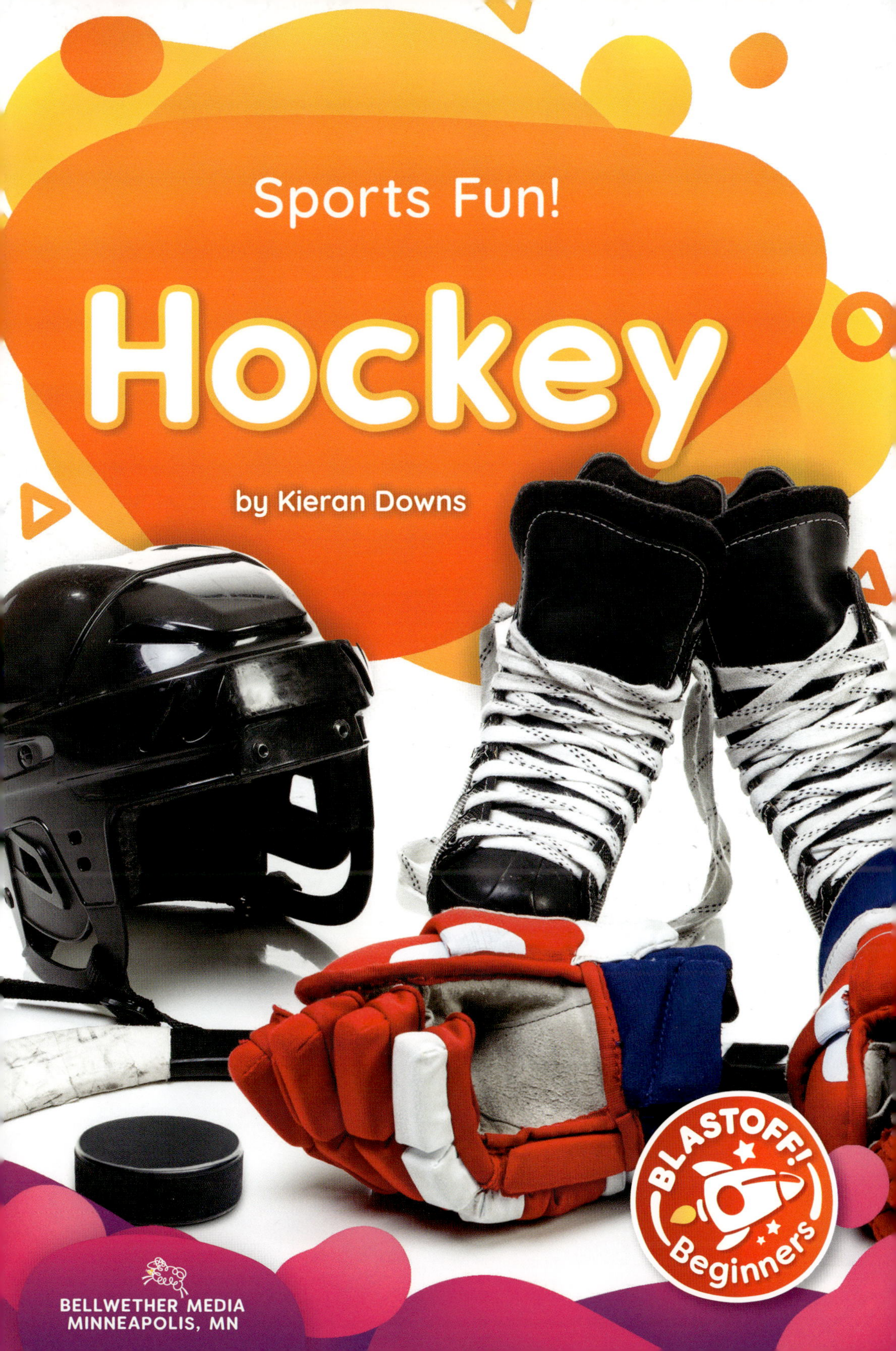
Sports Fun!
Hockey
by Kieran Downs
BLASTOFF! Beginners
BELLWETHER MEDIA
MINNEAPOLIS, MN

Blastoff! Beginners are developed by literacy experts and educators to meet the needs of early readers. These engaging informational texts support young children as they begin reading about their world. Through simple language and high frequency words paired with crisp, colorful photos, Blastoff! Beginners launch young readers into the universe of independent reading.

Sight Words in This Book

a	have	our	to
an	in	play	two
at	is	the	up
for	it	they	use
get	more	this	we
has	on	time	

This edition first published in 2024 by Bellwether Media, Inc.

Library of Congress Cataloging-in-Publication Data

Names: Downs, Kieran, author.
Title: Hockey / Kieran Downs.
Description: Minneapolis, MN : Bellwether Media, [2024] | Series: Sports fun! | Includes bibliographical references and index. | Audience: Ages 4-7 | Audience: Grades K-1
Identifiers: LCCN 2023004972 (print) | LCCN 2023004973 (ebook) | ISBN 9798886873955 (library binding) | ISBN 9798886875836 (ebook)
Subjects: LCSH: Hockey--Juvenile literature.
Classification: LCC GV847.25 .D68 2024 (print) | LCC GV847.25 (ebook) | DDC 796.962--dc23 eng/20230201
LC record available at https://lccn.loc.gov/2023004972
LC ebook record available at https://lccn.loc.gov/2023004973

Editor: Rebecca Sabelko Designer: Jeffrey Kollock

Printed in the United States of America, North Mankato, MN.

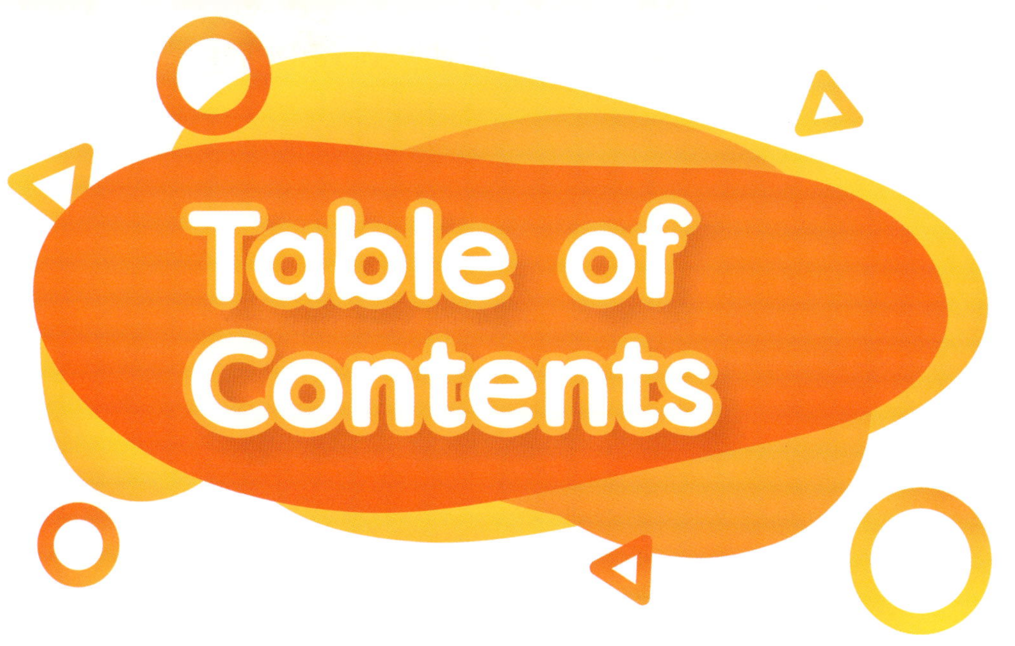
Table of Contents

We tie
our **skates**.
It is time
for hockey!

24
28

What Is Hockey?

Hockey is a team sport. Teams have six players.

team

Two teams
play in a game.
They play
on an **ice rink**.

ice rink

Teams try
to get **goals**.

On the Ice Rink

Players
wear skates.
They wear pads.

pads

Players use sticks. They move the **puck**. They pass to teammates.

stick

They shoot
the puck
at the net.

net

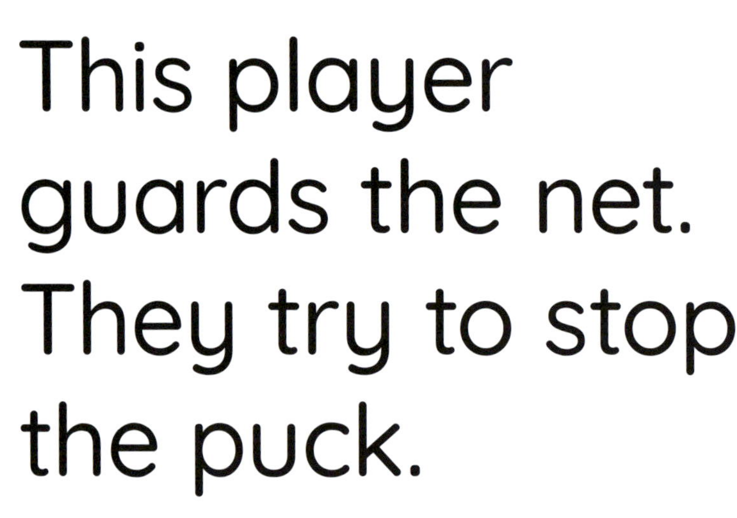

This player guards the net. They try to stop the puck.

Time is up.
This team has
more goals.
They win!

Hockey Facts

Playing Hockey

Hockey Moves

skate

pass

shoot

Glossary

goals

points scored in hockey

puck

a flat, round item used to score in hockey

ice rink

the place where hockey is played

skates

shoes with metal blades that are used to move on ice

To Learn More

ON THE WEB

FACTSURFER

Factsurfer.com gives you a safe, fun way to find more information.

1. Go to www.factsurfer.com.
2. Enter "hockey" into the search box and click 🔍.
3. Select your book cover to see a list of related content.

Index

The images in this book are reproduced through the courtesy of: Ronnie Chua, front cover, p. 3; Shell114, p. 4 (skates); Lucky Business, pp. 5, 11, 21; Hero Images Inc, pp. 7, 22 (shoot); Sergey Sprinyuk, p. 8; Pavel L Photo and Video, pp. 9, 22 (pass), 23 (ice rink); Anton Vierietin, p. 12; Fifoprod, p. 13; Ekaterina43, p. 14 (puck); Jim West, p. 15; Hero Images, p. 17; Lorraine Swanson, p. 19; Dardalnna, p. 22 (playing hockey, skate); anton5146, p. 23 (goals); Vaclav Volrab, p. 23 (puck); MCRMfotos, p. 23 (skates).